W9-AWZ-571

CONTENTS

pg. 32

pg. 20

pg. 72

Slow Cooking Tips

Sizes of CROCK-POT® Slow Cookers

Smaller **CROCK-POT®** slow cookers—such as 1- to 3½-quart models—are the perfect size for cooking for singles, a couple or empty nesters (and also for serving dips).

While medium-size **CROCK-POT®** slow cookers (those holding somewhere between 3 quarts and 5 quarts) will easily cook enough food at a time to feed a small family. They are also convenient for holiday side dishes or appetizers.

Large **CROCK-POT®** slow cookers are great for large family dinners, holiday entertaining and potluck suppers. A 6- to 7-quart model is ideal if you like to make meals in advance, or have dinner tonight and store leftovers for another day.

Types of CROCK-POT® Slow Cookers

Current **CROCK-POT®** slow cookers come equipped with many different features and benefits, from auto cook programs to oven-safe stoneware to timed programming. Please visit **WWW.CROCK-POT.COM** to find the **CROCK-POT®** slow cooker that best suits your needs.

How you plan to use a **CROCK-POT®** slow cooker may affect the model you choose to purchase. For everyday cooking, choose a size large enough to serve your family. If you plan to use the **CROCK-POT®** slow cooker primarily for entertaining, choose one of the larger sizes. Basic **CROCK-POT®** slow cookers can hold as little as 16 ounces or as much as 7 quarts. The smallest sizes are great for keeping dips warm on a buffet, while the larger sizes can more readily fit large quantities of food and larger roasts.

Cooking, Stirring and Food Safety

CROCK-POT® slow cookers are safe to leave unattended. The outer heating base may get hot as it cooks, but it should not pose a fire hazard. The heating element in the heating base functions at a low wattage and is safe for your countertops.

Your **CROCK-POT®** slow cooker should be filled about one-half to three-fourths full for most recipes unless otherwise instructed. Lean meats such as chicken or pork tenderloin will cook faster than meats with more connective tissue and fat such as beef chuck or pork shoulder. Bone-in meats will take longer than boneless cuts. Typical **CROCK-POT®** slow cooker dishes take approximately 7 to 8 hours to reach the simmer point on LOW and about 3 to 4 hours on HIGH. Once the vegetables and meat start to simmer and braise, their flavors will fully blend and meat will become fall-off-the-bone tender.

According to the U.S. Department of Agriculture, all bacteria are killed at a temperature of 165°F. It's important to follow the recommended cooking times and not to open the lid often, especially early in the cooking process when heat is building up inside the unit. If you need to open the lid to check on your food or are adding additional ingredients, remember to allow additional cooking time if necessary to ensure food is cooked through and tender.

Large **CROCK-POT®** slow cookers, the 6- to 7-quart sizes, may benefit from a quick stir halfway through cook time to help distribute heat and promote even cooking. It's usually unnecessary to stir at all, as even ½ cup liquid will help to distribute heat and the stoneware is the perfect medium for holding food at an even temperature throughout the cooking process.

Oven-Safe Stoneware

All **CROCK-POT**® slow cooker removable stoneware inserts may (without their lids) be used safely in ovens at up to 400°F. In addition, all **CROCK-POT**® slow cookers are microwavable without their lids. If you own another slow cooker brand, please refer to your owner's manual for specific stoneware cooking medium tolerances.

Frozen Food

Frozen food can be successfully cooked in a **CROCK-POT**® slow cooker. However, it will require longer cooking time than the same recipe made with fresh food. It's almost always preferable to thaw frozen food prior to placing it in the **CROCK-POT**® slow cooker. Using an instant-read thermometer is recommended to ensure meat is fully cooked through.

Pasta and Rice

If you are converting a recipe for a **CROCK-POT**® slow cooker that calls for uncooked pasta, first cook the pasta on the stovetop just until slightly tender. Then add the pasta to the **CROCK-POT**® slow cooker. If you are converting a recipe for the **CROCK-POT**® slow cooker that calls for cooked rice, stir in raw rice with the other recipe ingredients plus ¼ cup extra liquid per ¼ cup of raw rice.

Beans

Beans must be softened completely before combining with sugar and/or acidic foods in the **CROCK-POT**® slow cooker. Sugar and acid have a hardening effect on beans and will prevent softening. Fully cooked canned beans may be used as a substitute for dried beans.

Vegetables

Root vegetables often cook more slowly than meat. Cut vegetables accordingly to cook at the same rate as meat—large or small or lean versus marbled—and place near the sides or bottom of the stoneware to facilitate cooking.

Herbs

Fresh herbs add flavor and color when added at the end of the cooking cycle; if added at the beginning, many fresh herbs' flavor will dissipate over long cook times. Ground and/or dried herbs and spices work well in slow cooking and may be added at the beginning of cook time. For dishes with shorter cook times, hearty fresh herbs such as rosemary and thyme hold up well. The flavor power of all herbs and spices can vary greatly depending on their particular strength and shelf life. Use chili powders and garlic powder sparingly, as these can sometimes intensify over the long cook times. Always taste the finished dish and correct seasonings including salt and pepper.

Liquids

It's not necessary to use more than ½ to 1 cup liquid in most instances since juices in meats and vegetables are retained more in slow cooking than in conventional cooking. Excess liquid can be cooked down and concentrated after slow cooking on the stovetop or by removing meat and vegetables from stoneware, stirring in one of the following thickeners and setting the **CROCK-POT®** slow cooker to HIGH. Cover; cook on HIGH for approximately 15 minutes or until juices are thickened.

FLOUR: All-purpose flour is often used to thicken soups or stews. Stir cold water into the flour in a small bowl until smooth. With the **CROCK-POT®** slow cooker on HIGH, whisk the flour mixture into the liquid in the **CROCK-POT®** slow cooker. Cover; cook on HIGH 15 minutes or until the mixture is thickened.

CORNSTARCH: Cornstarch gives sauces a clear, shiny appearance; it's used most often for sweet dessert sauces and stir-fry sauces. Stir cold water into the cornstarch in a small bowl until the cornstarch dissolves. Quickly stir this mixture into the liquid in the **CROCK-POT®** slow cooker; the sauce will thicken as soon as the liquid simmers. Cornstarch breaks down with too much heat, so never add it at the beginning of the slow cooking process and turn off the heat as soon as the sauce thickens.

ARROWROOT: Arrowroot (or arrowroot flour) comes from the root of a tropical plant that is dried and ground to a powder; it produces a thick, clear sauce. Those who are allergic to wheat often use it in place of flour. Place arrowroot in a small bowl or cup and stir in cold water until the mixture is smooth. Quickly stir this mixture into the liquid in the **CROCK-POT®** slow cooker. Arrowroot thickens below the boiling point, so it even works well in a **CROCK-POT®** slow cooker on LOW. Too much stirring can break down an arrowroot mixture.

TAPIOCA: Tapioca is a starchy substance extracted from the root of the cassava plant. Its greatest advantage is that it withstands long cooking, making it an ideal choice for slow cooking. Add it at the beginning of cooking and you'll get a clear, thickened sauce in the finished dish. Dishes using tapioca as a thickener are best cooked on the LOW setting; tapioca may become stringy when boiled for a long time.

Milk

Milk, cream and sour cream break down during extended cooking. When possible, add them during the last 15 to 30 minutes of slow cooking, until just heated through. Condensed soups may be substituted for milk and may cook for extended times.

Fish

Fish is delicate and should be stirred into the **CROCK-POT®** slow cooker gently during the last 15 to 30 minutes of cooking time. Cover; cook just until cooked through and serve immediately.

Baked Goods

If you wish to prepare bread, cakes or pudding cakes in a **CROCK-POT®** slow cooker, you may want to purchase a covered, vented metal cake pan accessory for your **CROCK-POT®** slow cooker. You can also use any straight-sided soufflé dish or deep cake pan that will fit into the stoneware of your unit. Baked goods can be prepared directly in the stoneware; however, they can be a little difficult to remove from the insert, so follow the recipe directions carefully.

pg. 64

JOYOUS APPETIZERS

Warm Blue Crab Bruschetta

Makes 16 servings

- 4 cups peeled, seeded and diced plum tomatoes
- 1 cup diced white onion
- ⅓ cup olive oil
- 2 tablespoons sugar
- 2 tablespoons balsamic vinegar
- 2 teaspoons minced garlic
- ½ teaspoon dried oregano
- 1 pound lump blue crabmeat, picked over for shells
- 1½ teaspoons kosher salt
- ½ teaspoon cracked black pepper
- ⅓ cup minced fresh basil
- 2 baguettes, sliced and toasted

1. Combine tomatoes, onion, oil, sugar, vinegar, garlic and oregano in **CROCK-POT®** slow cooker; stir to blend. Cover; cook on LOW 2 hours.

2. Stir crabmeat, salt and pepper into **CROCK-POT®** slow cooker, taking care not to break up crabmeat. Cover; cook on LOW 1 hour. Fold in basil. Serve on toasted baguette slices.

Serving Suggestion: Crab topping can also be served on Melba toast or whole grain crackers.

Chablis-Infused Swiss Fondue

Makes 6 to 8 servings

3 cups dry Chablis or other white wine

2 teaspoons lemon juice

½ teaspoon grated lemon peel

6 cups (24 ounces) Swiss cheese, shredded

3 tablespoons all-purpose flour

3 tablespoons kirsch or cherry brandy

1 teaspoon mace, freshly ground

1 teaspoon black pepper

½ teaspoon paprika

Assorted cut-up fresh vegetables and Italian bread cubes

1. Heat wine, lemon juice and lemon peel in large saucepan over medium-high heat; bring to a simmer.

2. Combine cheese and flour in medium bowl. Gradually add cheese to saucepan, stirring constantly, until cheese is completely melted. Add kirsch; stir well to combine. Add mace, pepper and paprika; stir thoroughly.

3. Pour cheese mixture into **CROCK-POT®** slow cooker. Cover; cook on HIGH 30 minutes. Turn **CROCK-POT®** slow cooker to LOW. Cover; cook on LOW 2 to 5 hours, stirring occasionally. Serve with vegetables and Italian bread.

Raspberry-Balsamic Glazed Meatballs

1 **bag (2 pounds) frozen fully cooked meatballs**

1 **cup raspberry preserves**

3 **tablespoons sugar**

3 **tablespoons balsamic vinegar**

1 **tablespoon plus 1½ teaspoons Worcestershire sauce**

¼ **teaspoon red pepper flakes**

1 **tablespoon grated fresh ginger (optional)**

1. Coat inside of **CROCK-POT®** slow cooker with nonstick cooking spray. Add frozen meatballs.

2. Combine preserves, sugar, vinegar, Worcestershire sauce and red pepper flakes in small microwavable bowl. Microwave on HIGH 45 seconds; stir. Microwave 15 seconds or until melted. Reserve ½ cup glaze in refrigerator. Pour remaining glaze mixture over meatballs; stir until well coated. Cover; cook on LOW 5 hours or on HIGH 2½ hours.

3. Stir in reserved glaze and ginger, if desired. Cook, uncovered, on HIGH 15 to 20 minutes or until thickened slightly, stirring occasionally.

Serving Suggestion: To serve as a main dish, toss with chopped green onions and serve over rice. Makes 8 main-dish servings.

Stuffed Baby Bell Peppers

1 tablespoon olive oil

½ onion, chopped

½ pound ground beef, chicken or turkey

½ cup cooked rice

3 tablespoons chopped fresh Italian parsley

2 tablespoons lemon juice

1 tablespoon dried dill weed

1 tablespoon tomato paste, divided

½ teaspoon salt

⅛ teaspoon black pepper

¼ cup chicken or beef broth

1 bag yellow and red baby bell peppers (about 2 dozen)

1. Heat oil in medium skillet over medium heat. Add onion; cook and stir 5 minutes or until translucent.

2. Add beef; brown 6 to 8 minutes, stirring to break up meat. Drain fat. Remove to large bowl. Add rice, parsley, lemon juice, dill, 1½ teaspoons tomato paste, salt and black pepper; mix well. Whisk broth and remaining 1½ teaspoons tomato paste in small bowl.

3. Cut lengthwise slit down side of each bell pepper; run under cold water to wash out seeds. Fill each bell pepper with 2 to 3 teaspoons meat mixture. Place filled bell peppers in **CROCK-POT®** slow cooker, filling side up. Add broth mixture. Cover; cook on LOW 5 hours or on HIGH 2½ hours.

Stewed Fig and Blue Cheese Dip

1 tablespoon olive oil

1 medium onion, chopped

½ cup port wine

1 package (6 ounces) dried Calimyrna figs, finely chopped, plus additional fig halves for garnish

½ cup orange juice

½ cup crumbled blue cheese, divided

1 tablespoon unsalted butter

Assorted crackers and grapes

1. Heat oil in small skillet over medium-high heat. Add onion; cook and stir 7 to 8 minutes or until light golden. Stir in port. Bring to a boil; cook 1 minute. Remove to 1½-quart **CROCK-POT®** "No Dial" slow cooker; stir in 1 package figs and orange juice.

2. Cover; heat 1 to 1½ hours or until figs are plump and tender. Stir in ¼ cup blue cheese and butter. Sprinkle with remaining blue cheese. Garnish with additional fig halves. Serve with crackers and grapes.

Sausage and Swiss Chard Stuffed Mushrooms

4 tablespoons olive oil, divided

½ pound bulk pork sausage

½ onion, finely chopped

2 cups chopped Swiss chard

¼ teaspoon dried thyme

2 tablespoons garlic-and-herb-flavored dry bread crumbs

1½ cups chicken broth, divided

½ teaspoon salt, divided

½ teaspoon black pepper, divided

2 packages (6 ounces *each*) cremini mushrooms, stemmed*

2 tablespoons grated Parmesan cheese

2 tablespoons chopped fresh Italian parsley

*Do not substitute white button mushrooms.

1. Coat inside of **CROCK-POT**® slow cooker with nonstick cooking spray. Heat 1 tablespoon oil in medium skillet over medium heat. Add sausage; cook and stir 6 to 8 minutes or until browned. Remove sausage to medium bowl using slotted spoon.

2. Add onion to skillet; cook and stir 3 minutes or until translucent, scraping up any browned bits from bottom of skillet. Stir in chard and thyme; cook 1 to 2 minutes or until chard is wilted. Remove from heat.

3. Stir in sausage, bread crumbs, 1 tablespoon broth, ¼ teaspoon salt and ¼ teaspoon pepper. Brush remaining 3 tablespoons oil over mushrooms. Season with remaining ¼ teaspoon salt and ¼ teaspoon pepper. Fill mushrooms evenly with stuffing.

4. Pour remaining broth into **CROCK-POT**® slow cooker. Arrange stuffed mushrooms in bottom. Cover; cook on HIGH 3 hours. To serve, remove mushrooms using slotted spoon; discard cooking liquid. Combine cheese and parsley in small bowl; sprinkle evenly over mushrooms.

Bacon-Wrapped Dates

4 ounces goat cheese or blue cheese

1 package (8 ounces) dried pitted dates

1 pound thick-cut bacon (about 11 slices), halved

1. Fill **CROCK-POT®** slow cooker with about ½-inch water. Spoon goat cheese evenly into centers of dates; close. Wrap half slice of bacon around each date; secure with toothpicks.

2. Heat large skillet over medium heat. Add wrapped dates; cook and turn 5 to 10 minutes until browned. Remove to **CROCK-POT®** slow cooker.

3. Cover; cook on LOW 2 to 3 hours. Remove toothpicks before serving.

Lemon & Garlic Shrimp

Makes 6 to 8 servings

1 pound large raw shrimp, peeled and deveined (with tails on)

½ cup (1 stick) unsalted butter, cubed

3 cloves garlic, crushed

2 tablespoons lemon juice

½ teaspoon paprika

Salt and black pepper

2 tablespoons finely chopped fresh Italian parsley

Crusty bread, sliced (optional)

1. Coat inside of **CROCK-POT**® slow cooker with nonstick cooking spray. Add shrimp, butter and garlic; mix well. Cover; cook on HIGH 1¼ hours.

2. Turn off heat. Stir in lemon juice, paprika, salt and pepper. Spoon shrimp and liquid into large serving bowl. Sprinkle with parsley. Serve with crusty bread for dipping, if desired.

Chicken Meatballs with Chipotle-Honey Sauce

2 pounds ground chicken

2 eggs, lightly beaten

⅓ cup plain dry bread crumbs

⅓ cup chopped fresh cilantro

3 tablespoons lime juice, divided

4 cloves garlic, minced

1 can (4 ounces) chipotle peppers in adobo sauce, divided

1½ teaspoons salt, divided

¾ cup honey

⅓ cup chicken broth

⅓ cup tomato paste

2 teaspoons Dijon mustard

1 tablespoon vegetable oil, plus additional as needed

1. Spray two baking sheets with nonstick cooking spray. Combine chicken, eggs, bread crumbs, cilantro, 2 tablespoons lime juice, garlic, 1 tablespoon adobo sauce and 1 teaspoon salt in large bowl. Shape into 48 meatballs. Place meatballs in single layer on prepared baking sheets. Cover with plastic wrap; refrigerate 1 hour.

2. Combine 2 to 3 chipotle peppers, honey, broth, tomato paste, mustard, remaining 1 tablespoon lime juice and ½ teaspoon salt in food processor or blender; blend until smooth. Pour sauce into **CROCK-POT®** slow cooker.

3. Heat 1 tablespoon oil in large skillet over medium-high heat. Working in batches, brown meatballs on all sides, adding additional oil as needed. Remove meatballs to **CROCK-POT®** slow cooker. Stir gently to coat all meatballs. Cover; cook on HIGH 3 to 4 hours or until meatballs are no longer pink in centers.

Hot Broccoli Cheese Dip

Makes about 6 cups

½ cup (1 stick) butter

6 stalks celery, sliced

2 onions, chopped

2 cans (4 ounces *each*) sliced mushrooms, drained

¼ cup plus 2 tablespoons all-purpose flour

2 cans (10¾ ounces *each*) condensed cream of celery soup, undiluted

5 to 6 ounces garlic cheese, cut into cubes

2 packages (10 ounces *each*) frozen broccoli

French bread slices, bell pepper strips, cherry tomatoes

1. Melt butter in large skillet over medium heat. Add celery, onions and mushrooms; cook and stir 5 to 7 minutes or until onions are translucent. Stir in flour; cook 2 to 3 minutes. Remove to **CROCK-POT**® slow cooker.

2. Stir in soup, cheese and broccoli. Cover; cook on HIGH 45 minutes or until cheese is melted, stirring every 15 minutes. Turn **CROCK-POT**® slow cooker to LOW. Cover; cook on LOW 2 to 4 hours. Serve warm with bread and vegetables.

MERRY MEATS

Italian Braised Short Ribs in Red Wine

Makes 4 to 6 servings

- **3 pounds beef short ribs, trimmed**
  Salt and black pepper
- **1 tablespoon vegetable oil, plus additional as needed**
- **2 onions, sliced**
- **2 packages (8 ounces *each*) cremini mushrooms, quartered**
- **2 cups dry red wine**
- **2 cups beef broth**
- **2 teaspoons Italian seasoning**
- **2 cloves garlic, minced**
  Mashed potatoes or polenta

1. Coat inside of **CROCK-POT®** slow cooker with nonstick cooking spray. Season short ribs with salt and pepper. Heat 1 tablespoon oil in large skillet over medium-high heat. Working in batches, brown ribs on all sides, adding additional oil as needed. Remove to **CROCK-POT®** slow cooker.

2. Return skillet to heat. Add onions; cook and stir 3 minutes or until translucent. Stir in mushrooms, wine, broth, Italian seasoning and garlic; bring to a simmer. Simmer 3 minutes; pour over short ribs. Cover; cook on LOW 10 to 12 hours or on HIGH 6 to 8 hours. Season with salt and pepper. Remove ribs and mushrooms to serving platter. Strain cooking liquid; serve with mashed potatoes and cooking liquid.

Beef Roast with Dark Rum Sauce

Makes 6 servings

1 teaspoon ground allspice

½ teaspoon salt

½ teaspoon black pepper

¼ teaspoon ground cloves

1 beef rump roast (about 3 pounds)*

2 tablespoons extra virgin olive oil

1 cup dark rum, divided

½ cup beef broth

2 cloves garlic, minced

2 whole bay leaves, broken in half

½ cup packed dark brown sugar

¼ cup lime juice

*Unless you have a 5-, 6- or 7-quart **CROCK-POT®** slow cooker, cut any roast larger than 2½ pounds in half so it cooks completely.

1. Combine allspice, salt, pepper and cloves in small bowl. Rub spices onto all sides of roast.

2. Heat oil in large skillet over medium heat. Brown beef on all sides, turning as it browns. Remove to **CROCK-POT®** slow cooker. Add ½ cup rum, broth, garlic and bay leaves. Cover; cook on LOW 1 hour.

3. Combine remaining ½ cup rum, brown sugar and lime juice in small bowl; stir to blend. Pour over roast. Cover; cook on LOW 4 to 6 hours.

4. Remove roast to large cutting board. Cover loosely with foil; let stand 10 to 15 minutes before slicing. Remove and discard bay leaves. Serve with sauce.

Holiday Ham

1 **bone-in cooked ham (about 5 to 7 pounds), trimmed***

16 **whole cloves**

1 **cup water**

1½ **teaspoons vegetable oil**

1 **shallot, chopped**

1 **jar (12 ounces) cherry preserves or currant jelly**

¾ **cup dried orange-flavored cranberries or raisins**

½ **cup packed brown sugar**

½ **cup orange juice**

½ **teaspoon dry mustard**

*Unless you have a 5-, 6- or 7-quart **CROCK-POT®** slow cooker, cut any meat larger than 2½ pounds in half so it cooks completely.

1. Score ham. Place 1 clove in center of each diamond. Pour water into **CROCK-POT®** slow cooker; add ham. Cover; cook on LOW 5 to 6 hours or on HIGH 2½ to 3 hours.

2. Heat oil in small saucepan over medium-high heat. Add shallot; cook and stir 2 to 3 minutes or until translucent. Stir in preserves, cranberries, brown sugar, orange juice and dry mustard. Reduce heat to medium; cook until sugar is dissolved.

3. Remove ham from **CROCK-POT®** slow cooker; drain liquid. Place ham back into **CROCK-POT®** slow cooker; pour preserve mixture over ham. Cover; cook on HIGH 10 to 20 minutes or until fruit plumps.

Wine-Braised Boneless Leg of Lamb

Makes about 8 servings

1½ cups beef broth

¼ cup all-purpose flour

2 tablespoons tomato paste

1 teaspoon dried mint

1 teaspoon dried basil

1 teaspoon dried oregano

1 teaspoon salt, divided

½ teaspoon garlic powder

½ teaspoon black pepper, divided

24 baby new potatoes (about 1 pound)

24 baby carrots

1 ounce dried porcini mushrooms (optional)

1 tablespoon olive oil

3 to 3½ pounds boneless leg of lamb, trimmed and tied*

1 large onion, thinly sliced

4 cloves garlic, thinly sliced

¾ cup dry red wine

Sprig fresh oregano (optional)

*Unless you have a 5-, 6- or 7-quart **CROCK-POT®** slow cooker, cut any roast larger than 2½ pounds in half so it cooks completely.

1. Coat inside of **CROCK-POT®** slow cooker with nonstick cooking spray. Combine broth, flour, tomato paste, mint, basil, dried oregano, ½ teaspoon salt, garlic powder and ¼ teaspoon pepper in medium bowl. Pour broth mixture into **CROCK-POT®** slow cooker. Add potatoes, carrots and mushrooms, if desired.

2. Heat oil in large skillet over medium-high heat. Season lamb with remaining ½ teaspoon salt and ¼ teaspoon pepper. Add to skillet; cook and turn 8 to 12 minutes or until well browned. Remove lamb to **CROCK-POT®** slow cooker on top of vegetables.

3. Return skillet to medium-high heat. Add onion and garlic; cook and stir 5 to 6 minutes or until onion is softened. Add wine. Bring to a boil; cook 2 minutes. Pour onion mixture over lamb. Cover; cook on LOW 8 to 9 hours or on HIGH 4 to 5 hours. Garnish with fresh oregano.

Roast Chicken with Peas, Prosciutto and Cream

Makes 6 servings

1 cut-up whole chicken (2½ pounds)

Salt and black pepper

5 ounces prosciutto, diced

1 white onion, finely chopped

½ cup dry white wine

1 package (10 ounces) frozen peas

½ cup whipping cream

2 tablespoons water

1½ tablespoons cornstarch

4 cups bow tie pasta, cooked and drained

1. Season chicken with salt and pepper. Combine chicken, prosciutto, onion and wine in **CROCK-POT**® slow cooker. Cover; cook on LOW 8 to 10 hours or on HIGH 3½ to 4 hours. Stir peas and cream into cooking liquid in **CROCK-POT**® slow cooker during last 30 minutes of cooking.

2. Remove chicken to large cutting board when cooked through. Carve into slices, discarding bones. Remove chicken to warm platter.

3. Stir water into cornstarch in small bowl until smooth. Whisk into cooking liquid in **CROCK-POT**® slow cooker. Cover; cook on HIGH 10 to 15 minutes or until thickened.

4. To serve, spoon pasta onto individual plates. Place chicken on pasta; top each portion with sauce.

Pork Roast with Currant Cherry Salsa

1½ teaspoons chili powder

¾ teaspoon salt

½ teaspoon garlic powder

½ teaspoon paprika

¼ teaspoon ground allspice

1 boneless pork loin roast (2 pounds)

Nonstick cooking spray

½ cup water

1 package (1 pound) frozen pitted dark cherries, thawed, drained and halved

¼ cup currants or dark raisins

1 teaspoon grated orange peel

1 teaspoon balsamic vinegar

⅛ to ¼ teaspoon red pepper flakes

1. Combine chili powder, salt, garlic powder, paprika and allspice in small bowl; stir to blend. Rub roast evenly with spice mixture, pressing spices into roast.

2. Spray large skillet with cooking spray; heat over medium-high heat. Add roast; cook 6 to 8 minutes or until browned on all sides. Remove to **CROCK-POT®** slow cooker.

3. Pour water into skillet, stirring to scrape up brown bits. Pour liquid into **CROCK-POT®** slow cooker around roast. Cover; cook on LOW 6 to 8 hours.

4. Remove roast to large cutting board. Cover loosely with foil; let stand 10 to 15 minutes. Strain juices from **CROCK-POT®** slow cooker; discard solids. Keep warm.

5. Turn **CROCK-POT®** slow cooker to HIGH. Add cherries, currants, orange peel, vinegar and red pepper flakes to **CROCK-POT®** slow cooker. Cover; cook on HIGH 30 minutes. Slice pork; spoon warm juices over meat. Serve with salsa.

Ham and Sage Stuffed Cornish Hens

Makes 4 servings

1 cup plus 3 tablespoons sliced celery, divided

1 cup sliced leek (white part only)

2 tablespoons butter, divided

¼ cup finely diced onion

¼ cup diced smoked ham or prosciutto

1 cup seasoned stuffing mix

1 cup chicken broth

1 tablespoon finely chopped fresh sage *or* 1 teaspoon ground sage

4 Cornish hens (about 1½ pounds *each*)

Salt and black pepper

1. Coat inside of **CROCK-POT**® slow cooker with nonstick cooking spray. Toss 1 cup celery and leek in **CROCK-POT**® slow cooker.

2. Melt 1 tablespoon butter in large nonstick skillet over medium heat. Add remaining 3 tablespoons celery, onion and ham. Cook 5 minutes or until onion is soft, stirring frequently. Stir in stuffing mix, broth and sage. Remove mixture to medium bowl.

3. Rinse hens and pat dry. Sprinkle inside and outside of each hen with salt and pepper. Gently spoon stuffing into cavities. Tie each hen's drumsticks together with kitchen string.

4. Melt remaining 1 tablespoon butter in same skillet over medium-high heat. Place 2 hens, breast sides down, in skillet; cook until skins brown, turning to brown all sides. Remove to **CROCK-POT**® slow cooker. Repeat with remaining hens. Cover; cook on LOW 5 to 6 hours or on HIGH 3 to 4 hours. Remove string; place hens on serving platter. Spoon cooking broth over hens.

Turkey with Chunky Cherry Relish

Makes 4 to 6 servings

1 bag (16 ounces) frozen dark cherries, coarsely chopped

1 can (about 14 ounces) diced tomatoes with jalapeño peppers

1 package (6 ounces) dried cherry-flavored cranberries or dried cherries, coarsely chopped

2 small onions, thinly sliced

1 small green bell pepper, chopped

½ cup packed brown sugar

2 tablespoons quick-cooking tapioca

1½ tablespoons salt

½ teaspoon ground cinnamon

½ teaspoon black pepper

1 bone-in turkey breast (2½ to 3 pounds)

2 tablespoons water

1 tablespoon cornstarch

1. Place cherries, tomatoes, cranberries, onions, bell pepper, brown sugar, tapioca, salt, cinnamon and black pepper in **CROCK-POT**® slow cooker; mix well.

2. Place turkey on top of cherry mixture. Cover; cook on LOW 7 to 8 hours or until temperature registers 170°F on meat thermometer inserted into thickest part of breast, not touching bone. Remove turkey from **CROCK-POT**® slow cooker. Cover loosely with foil to keep warm.

3. Turn **CROCK-POT**® slow cooker to HIGH. Stir water into cornstarch in small bowl until smooth. Whisk cornstarch mixture into cherry mixture. Cook, uncovered, on HIGH 15 minutes or until sauce is thickened. Slice turkey; top with relish.

Slow Cooker Turkey Breast

½ to 1 teaspoon garlic powder

½ to 1 teaspoon paprika

1 boneless turkey breast (4 to 6 pounds)*

1 tablespoon dried parsley flakes

*Unless you have a 5-, 6- or 7-quart **CROCK-POT**® slow cooker, cut any piece of meat larger than 2½ pounds in half so it cooks completely.

1. Combine garlic powder and paprika in small bowl; rub onto turkey. Place turkey in **CROCK-POT**® slow cooker. Sprinkle with parsley flakes. Cover; cook on LOW 6 to 8 hours or on HIGH 2½ to 3 hours.

2. Remove turkey to large cutting board. Cover loosely with foil; let stand 10 to 15 minutes before slicing.

Pork Roast Landaise

2 tablespoons olive oil

2½ pounds boneless, center-cut pork loin roast

Salt and black pepper

1 medium onion, diced

2 cloves garlic, minced

2 parsnips, cut into ¾-inch slices

2 teaspoons dried thyme

¼ cup sugar

¼ cup red wine vinegar

½ cup port or dry sherry wine

2 cups chicken broth, divided

2 tablespoons cornstarch

3 pears, cored and sliced ¾ inch thick

1½ cups pitted prunes

1. Heat oil in large saucepan over medium-high heat. Season pork roast with salt and pepper; brown roast on all sides. Remove roast to **CROCK-POT®** slow cooker.

2. Add onion and garlic to saucepan. Reduce heat to medium; cook and stir 2 to 3 minutes. Stir in parsnips and thyme. Remove to **CROCK-POT®** slow cooker.

3. Combine sugar and vinegar in same saucepan; cook and stir 5 minutes or until mixture is thickened. Add port; cook 1 minute. Add 1¾ cups broth. Stir remaining ¼ cup broth into cornstarch in small bowl until smooth. Whisk into sauce and cook until smooth and slightly thickened.

4. Pour onion mixture into **CROCK-POT®** slow cooker. Cover; cook on LOW 8 hours or on HIGH 4 hours. Add pears and prunes during last 30 minutes of cooking.

SATISFYING SIDE DISHES

Fresh Berry Compote

Makes 4 servings

- **2 cups fresh blueberries**
- **4 cups fresh sliced strawberries**
- **2 tablespoons orange juice**
- **½ to ¾ cup sugar**

- **4 slices (½×1½ inches) lemon peel with no white pith**
- **1 whole cinnamon stick or ½ teaspoon ground cinnamon**

1. Place blueberries in **CROCK-POT®** slow cooker. Cover; cook on HIGH 45 minutes or until blueberries begin to soften.

2. Add strawberries, orange juice, ½ cup sugar, lemon peel and cinnamon stick; stir to blend. Cover; cook on HIGH 1 to 1½ hours or until strawberries soften and sugar dissolves. Check for sweetness and add more sugar if necessary, cooking until added sugar dissolves. Remove insert from **CROCK-POT®** slow cooker to heatproof surface; let cool.

 Fresh Fruit Topping: Carefully spoon out fruit, leaving cooking liquid in **CROCK-POT®** slow cooker. Stir ¼ cup cold water into 1 to 2 tablespoons cornstarch in small bowl until smooth; whisk into cooking liquid. Cover; cook on HIGH 10 to 15 minutes or until thickened. Return fruit to sauce; stir to blend.

Orange-Spiced Sweet Potatoes

2 pounds sweet potatoes, diced

½ cup packed dark brown sugar

½ cup (1 stick) butter, cubed

1 teaspoon ground cinnamon

1 teaspoon vanilla

½ teaspoon salt

½ teaspoon ground nutmeg

½ teaspoon grated orange peel

Juice of 1 medium orange

Chopped toasted pecans*

*To toast pecans, spread in single layer in small heavy skillet. Cook and stir over medium heat 1 to 2 minutes or until nuts are lightly browned.

Combine potatoes, brown sugar, butter, cinnamon, vanilla, salt, nutmeg, orange peel and juice in **CROCK-POT®** slow cooker; stir to blend. Cover; cook on LOW 4 hours or on HIGH 2 hours. Sprinkle with pecans.

Variation: For creamier potatoes, add ¼ cup milk or whipping cream and beat with electric mixer at medium speed until smooth. Sprinkle with the pecans.

Green Bean Casserole

2 packages (10 ounces *each*) frozen green beans

1 can (10¾ ounces) condensed cream of mushroom soup, undiluted

1 tablespoon chopped fresh Italian parsley

1 tablespoon chopped roasted red peppers

1 teaspoon dried sage

½ teaspoon salt

½ teaspoon black pepper

¼ teaspoon ground nutmeg

½ cup toasted slivered almonds*

*To toast almonds, spread in single layer in small heavy skillet. Cook and stir over medium heat 1 to 2 minutes or until nuts are lightly browned.

Combine beans, soup, parsley, red peppers, sage, salt, black pepper and nutmeg in **CROCK-POT**® slow cooker; stir to blend. Cover; cook on LOW 3 to 4 hours. Sprinkle with almonds.

Deluxe Potato Casserole

1 can (10¾ ounces) condensed cream of chicken soup, undiluted

1 container (8 ounces) sour cream

¼ cup chopped onion

¼ cup (½ stick) plus 3 tablespoons melted butter, divided

1 teaspoon salt

2 pounds red potatoes, peeled and diced

2 cups (8 ounces) shredded Cheddar cheese

1½ to 2 cups stuffing mix

1. Coat inside of **CROCK-POT®** slow cooker with nonstick cooking spray. Combine soup, sour cream, onion, ¼ cup butter and salt in small bowl; stir to blend.

2. Combine potatoes and cheese in **CROCK-POT®** slow cooker. Pour soup mixture over potato mixture; mix well. Sprinkle stuffing mix over potato mixture; drizzle with remaining 3 tablespoons butter. Cover; cook on LOW 8 to 10 hours or on HIGH 5 to 6 hours.

Tarragon Carrots in White Wine

Makes 6 to 8 servings

8 medium carrots, cut into matchsticks

½ cup chicken broth

½ cup dry white wine

1 tablespoon lemon juice

1 tablespoon minced fresh tarragon

2 teaspoons finely chopped green onions

1½ teaspoons chopped fresh Italian parsley

1 clove garlic, minced

1 teaspoon salt

2 tablespoons Melba toast, crushed

2 tablespoons cold water

1. Combine carrots, broth, wine, lemon juice, tarragon, green onions, parsley, garlic and salt in **CROCK-POT®** slow cooker; stir to blend. Cover; cook on LOW 2½ to 3 hours or on HIGH 1½ to 2 hours.

2. Dissolve toast crumbs in water in small bowl; add to carrots. Cover; cook on LOW 10 minutes or until thickened.

Lemon-Mint Red Potatoes

Makes 4 servings

2 pounds new red potatoes	¼ teaspoon black pepper
3 tablespoons extra virgin olive oil	4 tablespoons chopped fresh mint, divided
1 teaspoon salt	2 tablespoons butter
½ teaspoon Greek seasoning or dried oregano	2 tablespoons lemon juice
¼ teaspoon garlic powder	1 teaspoon grated lemon peel

1. Coat inside of **CROCK-POT®** slow cooker with nonstick cooking spray. Add potatoes and oil, stirring gently to coat. Sprinkle with salt, Greek seasoning, garlic powder and pepper. Cover; cook on LOW 7 hours or on HIGH 4 hours.

2. Stir in 2 tablespoons mint, butter, lemon juice and lemon peel until butter is completely melted. Cover; cook on HIGH 15 minutes. Sprinkle with remaining 2 tablespoons mint.

Tip: It's easy to prepare these potatoes ahead of time. Simply follow the recipe and then turn off the heat. Let it stand at room temperature for up to 2 hours. You may reheat or serve the potatoes at room temperature.

Sweet Potato and Pecan Casserole

Makes 6 to 8 servings

1 can (40 ounces) sweet potatoes, drained and mashed

½ cup apple juice

⅓ cup plus 2 tablespoons butter, melted and divided

½ teaspoon salt

½ teaspoon ground cinnamon

¼ teaspoon black pepper

2 eggs, beaten

⅓ cup chopped pecans

⅓ cup packed brown sugar

2 tablespoons all-purpose flour

1. Combine potatoes, apple juice, ⅓ cup butter, salt, cinnamon and pepper in large bowl; beat in eggs. Pour mixture into **CROCK-POT®** slow cooker.

2. Combine pecans, brown sugar, flour and remaining 2 tablespoons butter in small bowl; stir to blend. Spread over sweet potatoes. Cover; cook on HIGH 3 to 4 hours.

Cheesy Mashed Potato Casserole

Makes 10 to 12 servings

4 pounds Yukon Gold potatoes, cut into 1-inch pieces

2 cups vegetable broth

3 tablespoons unsalted butter, cubed

½ cup milk, heated

⅓ cup sour cream

2 cups (8 ounces) shredded sharp Cheddar cheese, plus additional for garnish

½ teaspoon salt

¼ teaspoon black pepper

Chopped fresh Italian parsley (optional)

1. Coat inside of **CROCK-POT®** slow cooker with nonstick cooking spray. Add potatoes and broth; dot with butter. Cover; cook on LOW 4½ to 5 hours.

2. Mash potatoes with potato masher; stir in milk, sour cream, 2 cups cheese, salt and pepper until cheese is melted. Garnish with additional cheese and parsley.

Rosemary-Olive Focaccia

Makes 1 loaf

1 cup warm water (100° to 110°F)

3 tablespoons extra virgin olive oil

3 packets (0.25 ounces *each*) active dry yeast

1 tablespoon sugar

3 cups all-purpose flour

½ cup pitted kalamata olives, chopped

1 tablespoon plus 1 to 2 teaspoons chopped fresh rosemary, divided

1 teaspoon salt

¼ teaspoon red pepper flakes (optional)

1. Combine water, oil, yeast and sugar in medium bowl; let stand 5 minutes. Combine flour, olives, 1 tablespoon rosemary and salt in large bowl. Pour water mixture into flour mixture; stir until rough dough forms. Turn dough out onto floured surface; knead about 5 to 6 minutes or until smooth. Place dough in oiled bowl, turning to coat surface. Cover with plastic wrap and let stand in a warm place about 1½ hours or until doubled in size.

2. Punch down dough. Coat inside of oval 6-quart **CROCK-POT®** slow cooker with nonstick cooking spray. Add dough; press down and stretch to fit. Sprinkle with remaining 1 to 2 teaspoons rosemary and red pepper flakes, if desired. Cover; cook on HIGH 1½ to 2 hours or until dough is puffed and lightly browned on the sides. Remove to wire rack; let cool 10 minutes before cutting into wedges.

YULETIDE DESSERTS

Pumpkin-Cranberry Custard

Makes 4 to 6 servings

1 can (30 ounces) pumpkin
  pie filling

1 can (12 ounces) evaporated
  milk

1 cup dried cranberries

4 eggs, beaten

1 cup whole gingersnap
  cookies (optional)

Combine pumpkin, evaporated milk, cranberries and eggs in **CROCK-POT®** slow cooker; stir to blend. Cover; cook on HIGH 4 to 4½ hours. Serve with gingersnaps, if desired.

Chocolate Chip Lemon Loaf

1²⁄₃ cups all-purpose flour
1½ teaspoons baking powder
¼ teaspoon salt
½ cup granulated sugar
½ cup shortening
2 eggs
½ cup milk

½ cup semisweet chocolate chips
Grated peel of 1 lemon
Juice of 1 lemon
¼ to ½ cup powdered sugar
Melted semisweet chocolate (optional)

1. Make foil handles using three 18×2-inch strips of heavy-duty foil or use regular foil folded to double thickness. Place in 5-quart **CROCK-POT®** slow cooker; crisscross foil to form spoke design across bottom and up sides. Prepare 2-quart casserole or soufflé dish that fits inside of **CROCK-POT®** slow cooker with nonstick cooking spray. Combine flour, baking powder and salt in medium bowl.

2. Beat granulated sugar and shortening in large bowl with electric mixer at medium-high speed until blended. Add eggs, one at a time, mixing well after each addition. Add flour mixture and milk alternately. Stir in chocolate chips and lemon peel.

3. Spoon batter into prepared casserole. Cover with greased foil. Place dish in **CROCK-POT®** slow cooker. Cover; cook on LOW 3 to 4 hours or on HIGH 1½ to 2 hours or until edges are golden and knife inserted into center of loaf comes out clean. Remove dish from **CROCK-POT®** slow cooker; remove foil. Cool completely on wire rack.

4. Combine lemon juice and ¼ cup powdered sugar in small bowl until smooth. Add more sugar as needed to reach desired glaze consistency. Pour glaze over loaf. Drizzle loaf with melted chocolate, if desired.

Triple Chocolate Fantasy

Makes 36 pieces

2 **pounds white almond bark, broken into pieces**

1 **bar (4 ounces) sweetened chocolate, broken into pieces***

1 **package (12 ounces) semisweet chocolate chips**

3 **cups coarsely chopped pecans, toasted****

*Use your favorite high-quality chocolate candy bar.

**To toast pecans, spread in single layer in heavy skillet. Cook and stir over medium heat 1 to 2 minutes or until nuts are lightly browned.

1. Place bark, sweetened chocolate and chocolate chips in **CROCK-POT®** slow cooker. Cover; cook on HIGH 1 hour. *Do not stir.*

2. Turn **CROCK-POT®** slow cooker to LOW. Cover; cook on LOW 1 hour, stirring every 15 minutes. Stir in nuts.

3. Drop mixture by tablespoonfuls onto baking sheet covered with waxed paper; cool. Store in tightly covered container.

Variations: Here are a few ideas for other imaginative items to add in along with or instead of the pecans: raisins; crushed peppermint candy, candy-coated baking bits, crushed toffee, peanuts or pistachio nuts, chopped gum drops, chopped dried fruit, candied cherries, chopped marshmallows or sweetened coconut.

Cherry Flan

5 eggs	1 teaspoon vanilla
½ cup sugar	1 bag (16 ounces) frozen pitted dark sweet cherries, thawed
½ teaspoon salt	
¾ cup all-purpose flour	
1 can (12 ounces) evaporated milk	Whipped cream or cherry vanilla ice cream

1. Coat inside of **CROCK-POT®** slow cooker with nonstick cooking spray. Beat eggs, sugar and salt in large bowl with electric mixer at high speed until thick and pale yellow. Add flour; beat until smooth. Beat in evaporated milk and vanilla.

2. Pour batter into **CROCK-POT®** slow cooker. Place cherries evenly over batter. Cover; cook on LOW 3½ to 4 hours or until flan is set. Serve warm with whipped cream.

Cinnamon Latté

Makes 6 to 8 servings

6 cups double-strength brewed coffee*	3 whole cinnamon sticks, plus additional for garnish
2 cups half-and-half	*Double the amount of coffee grounds normally used to brew coffee. Or substitute 8 teaspoons instant coffee dissolved in 6 cups boiling water.
1 cup sugar	
1 teaspoon vanilla	

1. Blend coffee, half-and-half, sugar and vanilla in 3- to 4-quart **CROCK-POT®** slow cooker. Add 3 cinnamon sticks. Cover; cook on HIGH 3 hours.

2. Remove and discard cinnamon sticks. Garnish each serving with additional cinnamon sticks.

Cherry Flan

Bananas Foster

12 bananas, cut into quarters	2 teaspoons rum
1 cup flaked coconut	1 teaspoon ground cinnamon
1 cup dark corn syrup	
⅔ cup butter, melted	½ teaspoon salt
¼ cup lemon juice	12 slices pound cake
2 teaspoons grated lemon peel	1 quart vanilla ice cream

1. Combine bananas and coconut in **CROCK-POT®** slow cooker. Combine corn syrup, butter, lemon juice, lemon peel, rum, cinnamon and salt in medium bowl; stir to blend. Pour corn syrup mixture over bananas.

2. Cover; cook on LOW 1 to 2 hours. To serve, arrange bananas on pound cake slices. Top with ice cream and warm sauce.

Viennese Coffee

3 cups strong freshly brewed hot coffee	⅓ cup whipping cream, plus additional for topping
3 tablespoons chocolate syrup	¼ cup crème de cacao or Irish cream
1 teaspoon sugar	Chocolate shavings (optional)

1. Combine coffee, chocolate syrup and sugar in **CROCK-POT®** slow cooker. Cover; cook on LOW 2 to 2½ hours.

2. Stir ⅓ cup whipping cream and crème de cacao into **CROCK-POT®** slow cooker. Cover; cook on LOW 30 minutes or until heated through. Ladle coffee into coffee cups. Top with additional whipped cream and chocolate shavings, if desired.

Bananas Foster

Chocolate Orange Fondue

½ cup whipping cream	⅓ cup orange liqueur
1½ tablespoons butter	¾ teaspoon vanilla
6 ounces 60 to 70% bittersweet chocolate, coarsely chopped	Marshmallows, strawberries and pound cake cubes

1. Bring cream and butter to a boil in medium saucepan over medium heat. Remove from heat. Stir in chocolate, liqueur and vanilla until chocolate is melted. Place over medium-low heat; cook and stir 2 minutes until smooth.

2. Coat inside of **CROCK-POT® LITTLE DIPPER®** slow cooker with nonstick cooking spray. Fill with warm fondue. Serve with marshmallows, strawberries and pound cake cubes.

Chai Tea Cherries 'n' Cream

2 cans (15½ ounces *each*) pitted cherries in pear juice

2 cups water

½ cup orange juice

1 cup sugar

4 cardamom pods

2 whole cinnamon sticks (broken in half)

1 teaspoon grated orange peel

¼ ounce coarsely chopped candied ginger

4 whole cloves

2 whole black peppercorns

4 green tea bags

1 container (6 ounces) black cherry yogurt

1 quart vanilla ice cream

Sprigs fresh mint (optional)

1. Drain cherries, reserving juice. Combine reserved pear juice, water and orange juice in **CROCK-POT®** slow cooker. Mix in sugar, cardamom pods, cinnamon sticks, orange peel, ginger, cloves and peppercorns. Cover; cook on HIGH 1½ hours.

2. Remove spices with slotted spoon and discard. Stir in tea bags and reserved cherries. Cover; cook on HIGH 30 minutes.

3. Turn off heat. Remove and discard tea bags. Remove cherries from liquid; set aside. Let liquid cool until just warm. Whisk in yogurt until smooth.

4. To serve, divide warm cherries and yogurt sauce among wine or cocktail glasses. Top each serving with ice cream; swirl lightly. Garnish with mint.

INDEX